HOW TO LIVE WITH A NEUROTIC WIFE

Books in this series published by New English Library
By Stephen Baker
HOW TO LIVE WITH A NEUROTIC HUSBAND
HOW TO LIVE WITH A NEUROTIC WIFE
GAMES DOGS PLAY

By Stephen Baker and Eric Gurney
HOW TO LIVE WITH A NEUROTIC DOG

By Eric Gurney
HOW TO LIVE WITH A CALCULATING CAT
THE CALCULATING CAT RETURNS

HOW TO LIVE WITH A NEUROTIC WIFE

by Stephen Baker

Illustrated by George Woodbridge

NEW ENGLISH LIBRARY

First published in the USA in 1970 by Doubleday & Company, Inc.

First published in Great Britain in 1970 by New English Library Limited

First NEL Paperback Edition October 1971
Reprinted October 1974
Reprinted October 1979
This new edition March 1983

NEL Books are published by
New English Library,
Mill Road, Dunton Green,
Sevenoaks, Kent.
Editorial office: 47 Bedford Square, London WC1B 3DP

**Made and printed in Great Britain by
Collins, Glasgow**

0 450 02151 3

Dedicated to all wives with a sense of humour.

CONTENTS

HOW TO LIVE WITH A NEUROTIC WIFE

CHAPTER I

UNDERSTANDING A NEUROTIC WIFE

You must, first of all, understand what makes your wife neurotic.

The answer is simple.

It's you.

Consider that possibility before you blithely dismiss it. As your wife, she is most likely to be married to you. Right away, she has a problem. She may be required to live with you under the same roof. Her surname—by a chain of circumstances—coincides with yours, making it more difficult than ever to keep her marriage a secret among friends and relatives. No wonder that, sooner or later, usually a day after the wedding, she becomes an obsessive-compulsive-depressive-passive-aggressive personality, more scientifically known as a nut.

Then, too, unconsciously you are giving her an inferiority complex. Standing next to you, she probably has to look up to you. She can't help noticing that your biceps are bigger, your nostrils more undulating, your incisors sharper, and your earlobes are wider than hers.

You can run faster.

You can hold your breath longer.

You can climb higher.

You can hang from a branch by one arm.

You can jump higher.

The striking resemblance between man and his predecessors, the primates, only confirms to the wife what she suspected all along: namely, that on the evolutionary ladder, she has long surpassed the male.

Woman's image of herself.

Soon, your wife will discover that under certain special circumstances she may be asked to stay in the same room with you, perhaps even with the lights turned off. Thus, she must learn to protect herself. This should be no problem, however, for nature endowed a woman with formidable tools to ward off her natural enemies, such as her male companion. She has arms, legs, elbows, knees, nails, and teeth made just for that purpose.

Then, too, she has vocal cords unique in the world of nature. While men prefer words as means of communication, women employ a wider and more imaginative range of sounds. They also hiss, whine, snort, moan, howl, roar, cackle, and use words they invent as they go along. With the aid of these sound effects they not only can stop the approaching adversary in his tracks but force him to go back faster than he came.

And that isn't all. Women also excel as throwers. Their aim is poor but their ability to heave objects across a room is not. Anyone staying in the immediate vicinity must do so at his own risk. Among the Identified Flying Objects (IFO) favoured by women are dishes, pillows, lamps, chairs, tables, pianos, and full-grown cats.

A woman's brain, much like the rest of her anatomy, differs noticeably from the male's. It makes up in complexity what it lacks in size. It has a number of hemispheres whose functions are not understood by scientists yet—or anyone else, for that matter.

(1) BACK-TALK CENTRE is part of speech control mechanism. (2) Producing excuses is the ALIBI CORTEX. (3) REFLEX MECHANISM sends messages to various parts of the body so that she can step on the gas pedal instead of the brake pedal (and vice versa), and shift car into reverse to move it forward. (4) ALTERNATING BRAIN CURRENT speeds mind-changing process. (5) To help her forget what she should have remembered, and remember what she should have forgotten, are the MEMORY CELLS. (6) EXTRA-SENSORY UNIT in her brain makes it possible for her to guess correctly where her husband was seen the evening before—and with whom

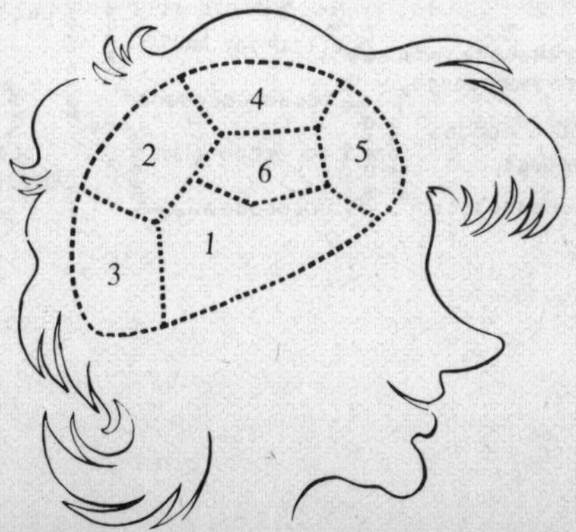

Complex structure of brain enables woman to follow a thought process unique to her species. For reasons clear only to her, she calls the thought process "logic".

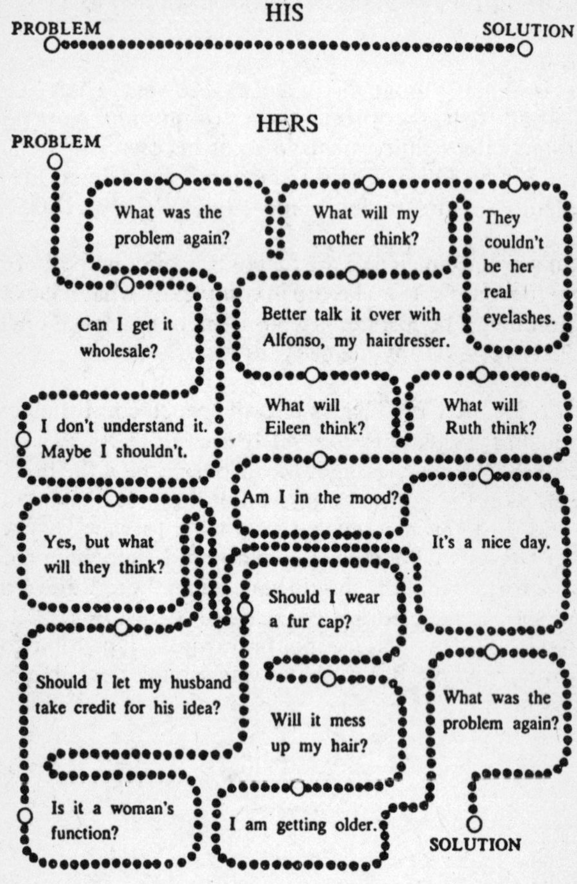

In all marriages there must be a display of love. A wife can expect that her husband should *demonstrate* his affection toward her now and then, as, for example, when he is with her on the bus, subway, or elevator; or when he talks to her, reads the newspaper, sits in the movies, walks, jogs, goes deep-sea diving. Remember that your wife married you for love. She loves everything about you: your house, automobile, swimming pool, bank account, and all tangible assets.

How long has it been since you surprised your wife with a peck on the cheek?

Have you ever demonstrated your love for her at the breakfast table?

Heart is the symbol of love. Use it as part of decor at home to reassure her of your affections.

CHAPTER II

THE ESCAPE MECHANISM OF A NEUROTIC WIFE

For practical reasons, if for no other, many wives cannot do what they would really like; that is, to get away from home and, most of all, their husbands. So they must settle for the next best thing, which is to dream of faraway places while not leaving the house.

The way by which this feat is accomplished is known among psychologists as *escape mechanism*.

Fortunately, women have active minds. The fact that they do not want to waste their time on painting murals, writing poetry, or working on mathematical formulas should not be confused with lack of true creative genius. As practical creatures, they simply prefer to spend their off-working hours—which is all day long—on more constructive undertakings, such as contemplation. There are probably millions of wives lying on their backs on living room couches all over the nation at this very minute, breathing heavily and thinking about life and what it could have been if only they were married to someone other than their husbands.

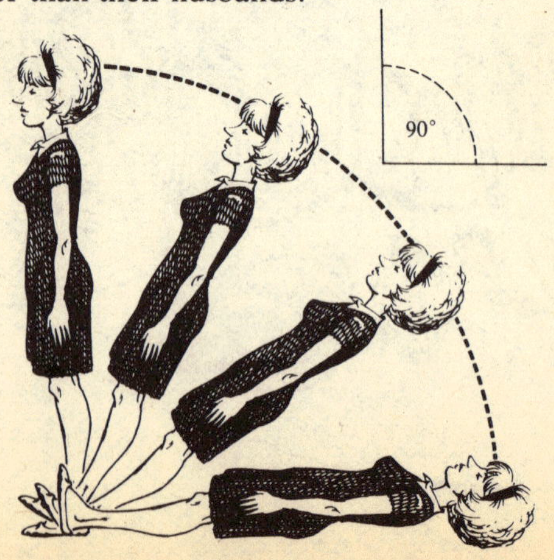

Most housewives favour a flat position for the purpose of deductive reasoning. This posture has several advantages. It allows blood supply to flow to the brain where there is presumably still some activity. It also helps to distribute weight and relieve feet from carrying the entire burden of the body. The quickest way to change from vertical (90°) to horizontal position (180°) is to fall backwards with arms held stiffly to sides, using heels as pivoting points. The manoeuvre takes only a few seconds and—thanks to earth's gravitational pull—it can be accomplished with a minimum of muscular effort.

THE THREE BASIC MEDITATIVE POSTURES

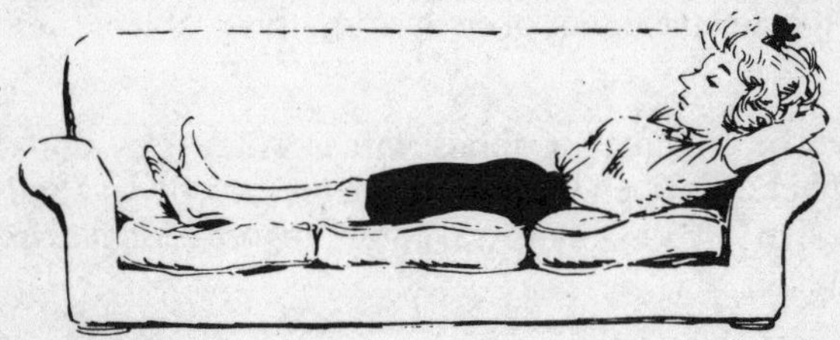

CLASSIC REPOSE is popular with beginners.

DROOPY DOZE is for the more accomplished thinkers.

SIDE ROLL is for those who like to have plenty of room to think.

There are women who do not accept daydreaming as a form of escape. They recognise the difference between fact and fancy; they believe only what they see with their own two eyes. For these sceptics, television was invented.

To be sure, television represented a hardship on women at first, for it necessitated their getting up several times a day to adjust switches and knobs. As time went on, the problem was eliminated by means of the remote control gadget. It weighs only a few ounces and can be held in one hand, freeing the other hand to stifle a yawn, pick the nose, or scratch the head. True, the thumb and forefinger still must be moved when pushing a button, but then there is hope that with the advancement of civilization this problem, too, will be solved.

Thus, it will be possible for a housewife to watch television with one or both of her eyes open (depending on the time of day) and remain on the couch all day long, save for an occasional trip to the bathroom.

Television set (A) in the living room should be located so as to permit uninterrupted viewing from any and all angles. Blinds (B) are drawn to keep down noise disturbance such as clatter of the lawnmower pushed back and forth by husband outside the house. Light (C) dims gradually as in a theatre. Mirrors (D and E) make it possible to watch television from kitchen. Chair (F) at the dining table faces the television set.

More than any other way, a woman achieves her greatest fulfilment in her dreams. Here she can be herself at last.

Since she spends most of her waking hours soundly asleep, a woman has more experience in dreaming than her husband. Hence, her fantasies are more colourful, more interesting, more complete.

So busy is she in her dreams, in fact, that more often than not she wakes up thoroughly exhausted. This explains why so many wives prefer to stay in bed in the morning while their husbands make breakfast for themselves.

It is important to remember, however, that a woman does not have to be asleep in order to dream. She is perfectly capable of dreaming with her eyes wide open while crossing the street against the red

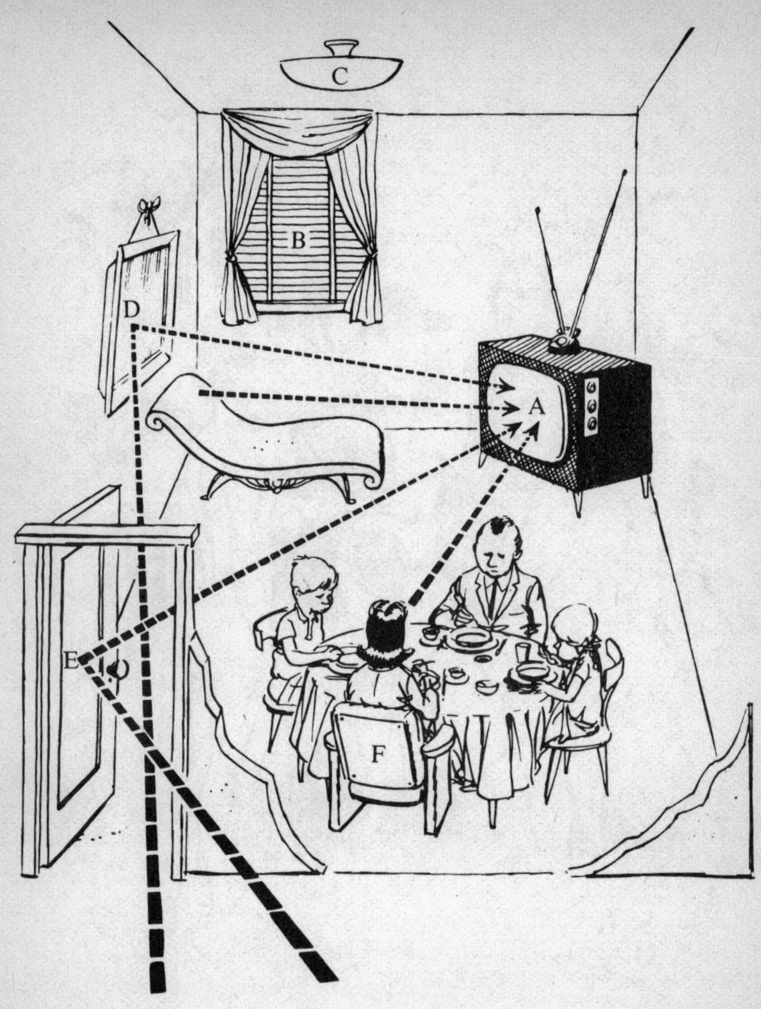

light, answering the policeman's questions, driving an automobile in heavy traffic, making out the family budget, balancing a cheque book, taking telephone messages for her husband, engaging in conversations with others, or entertaining the boss at home.

The following pages show the kind of dreams that can occur to any normal neurotic wife—including perhaps your own.

DREAM No. 1 "I am the social director in a nudist colony"

DREAM No. 2 "I am an anthropologist studying the mating habits of a polyandrous tribe"

DREAM No. 3 "I am the widow of the world's richest man"

DREAM No. 4 "I am a furrier's mistress"

DREAM No. 5
"I am being serenaded by my husband conducting the New York Philharmonic Orchestra"

DREAM No. 6 "I am the only girl in the lifeboat"

CHAPTER III

SHARING THE BEDROOM WITH A NEUROTIC WIFE

There are times when you must share the bedroom, or even your bed, with your wife. This of course brings up a multitude of problems.

The reason is that there is a fundamental difference of opinions between the sexes as to the intent of a bedroom. Husbands think of it as a place to display affections and promptly go to sleep afterwards. To a wife, a bedroom has other, more subtle meanings.

For her, a bedroom is an enclosure designed primarily for the purpose of talking things over. It has four walls and the acoustics make arguments sound more imposing. The husband is cornered at last. There is no way he can leave the premises without attracting her attention. And he just can't jump out of bed and take a walk around the block wearing only his pyjamas or less.

To make bedrooms even more practical for her use, there are beds in them. This piece of furniture represents a utilitarian item to a husband, but not to a wife. To her, a bed is at once a playground, an analyst's couch, a soap box, a camping ground, an athletic field, and a place to hold meetings with her as the Main Speaker.

Trying to get away from it all, many husbands spend their nights in twin beds. Others, in an attempt to get out of hearing distance altogether, establish residence in separate sleeping quarters. Neither of these solutions is completely satisfactory, however, for it makes love-making a complicated—and sometimes impossible—undertaking.

Less radical methods prove to be more workable. Hiding under the blanket or mattress offers temporary relief. Even more effective is use of the so-called Murphy bed which swings up against the wall at a mere pull of a lever. This type of bed, however, requires agility and quick reflexes. You must be able to roll out of it before it starts moving upwards lest you find yourself flattened against the wall in a vertical position—and still very much next to your spouse.

Sharing the same bed can become a source of controversy between the two interested parties. Both need room to sleep comfortably. As in all human relationships, your sense of fair play should be your Sharing the same bed can become a source of controversy between the two interested parties. Both need room to sleep comfortably. As in all human relationships, your sense of fair play should be your guide. Use jurisdictional standards as they apply to property rights between husband and wife; i.e., ninety per cent of the estate goes to her, ten per cent to you.

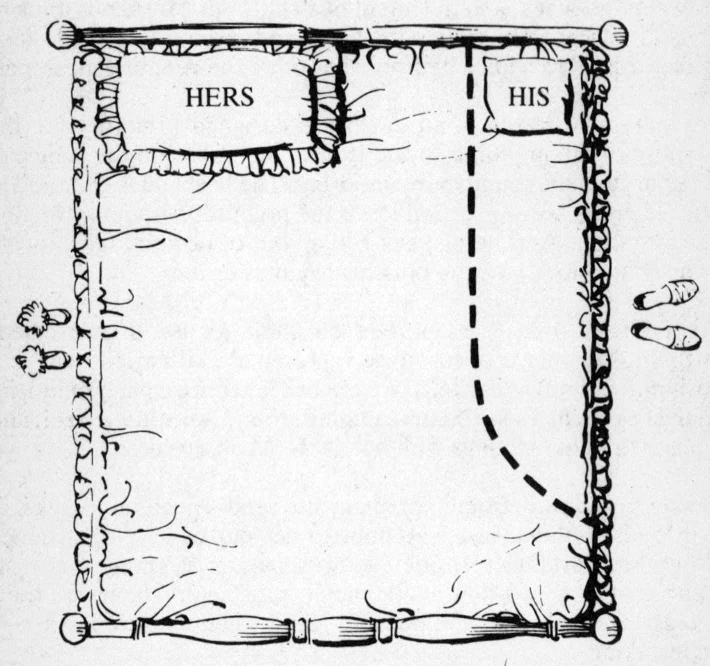

HIS IDEA

Wives like to improve the appearance of a bed. They think of it as an extension of a personality; namely, their own. This may confuse the husband who looks for comfort, but that is his problem, not hers.

HER IDEA

Staying in bed with a neurotic wife calls for athletic prowess, a well-developed sense of balance, and, most of all, the ability to answer questions while fast asleep.

Not all neurotic wives conduct themselves the same way in bed. Shown on the following pages are more typical nocturnal behaviour patterns.

THE LATE LATE READER catches up on her reading after midnight. She has a keen sense of humour and shakes the bed with her laughter. Grab side of the bed to stay atop.

BLANKET GATHERER is most active on cold nights. Try sleeping in your overcoat, mittens, earmuffs, and two pairs of woollen socks.

SHORT ORDER COOK turns on electric blanket to "high" on hot summer nights. Give her the blanket; keep the fan for yourself.

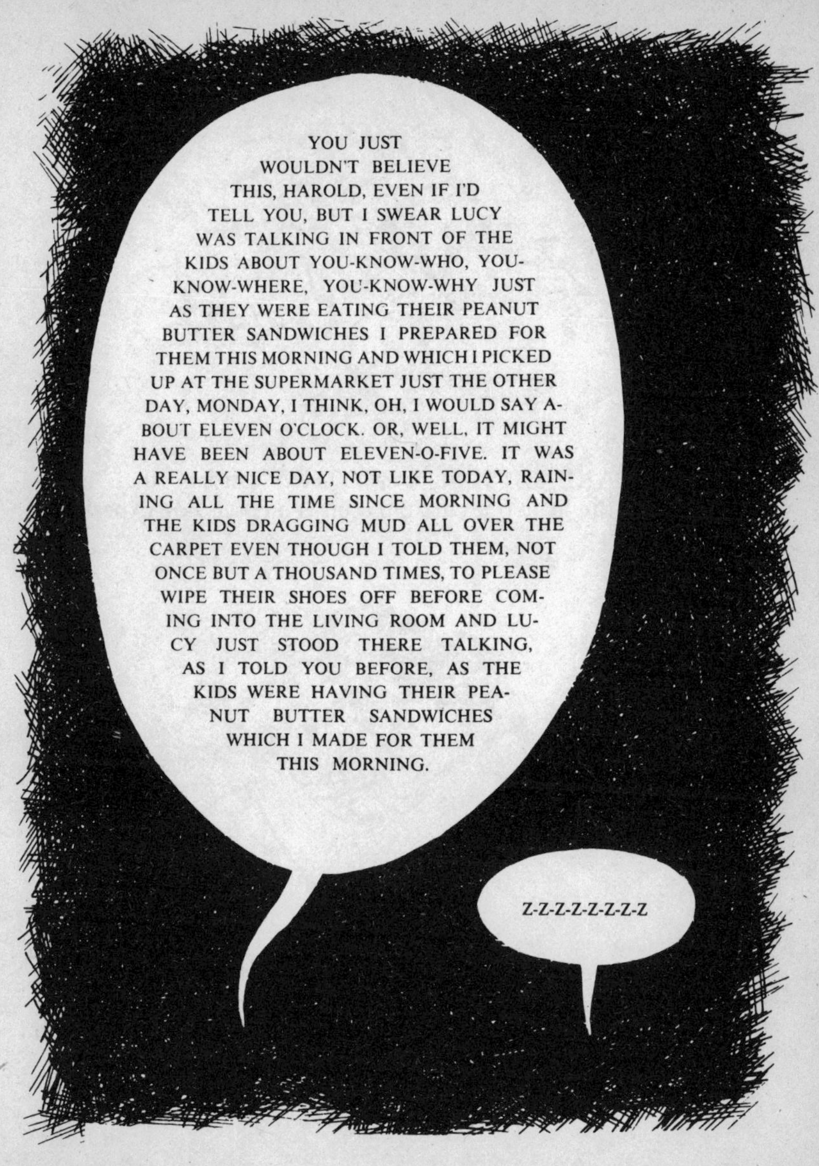

BEDTIME STORY TELLER comes alive at the end of the day—or night.

THE KIDS-ARE-SUCH-FUN MOTHER insists that being awakened by the little ones at 5.30 a.m. is a rewarding experience for any parent.

SNUGGLER becomes more social late at night. She envelops you with her arms and legs, pinning your body firmly to the mattress. When numbness sets in, try tossing your way to freedom, or push your knee against her belly.

Wife's alibis for awakening you are as varied as her ways of leaving the bed:

1. IS THAT JIMMY CRYING?
2. I THINK I'LL FIX MYSELF A VIRGINIA HAM SANDWICH WITH TURKEY, MELTED SWISS CHEESE ON FRENCH TOAST WITH SOME MAPLE SYRUP.
3. WOULD YOU LIKE A COCKTAIL, DEAR?
4. LISTEN TO THOSE CRICKETS, HOW CAN ANYONE GO TO SLEEP WITH ALL THAT NOISE?
5. WHAT TIME IS IT?
6. I THINK I'LL OPEN THE WINDOWS.
7. I THINK I'LL CLOSE THE WINDOWS.
8. HOW COME YOU'RE NOT SNORING? YOU'RE DEAD, OR SOMETHING?
9. I'M GOING TO READ.
10. I'M TAKING THE DOG OUT FOR A WALK. FRESH AIR WILL DO HIM GOOD.
11. I'M GOING TO TAKE A LOOK AT THE FULL MOON. OKAY WITH YOU?
12. ARE YOU ASLEEP, DEAR?
13. IT'S DARK IN HERE.

THE I-HAVE-TO-GET-UP-JUST-FOR-ONE-MINUTE-DEAR bed companion wakes you up just when you are about to fall asleep. She makes her exit gingerly sliding over your body, stepping on your face for support.

THE LAMP LIGHTER turns on the light *before* she steps on your face, not after.

TOE-PAINTER turns bed into a beauty parlour, lining up bottles, jars, nail clippers, files, scissors, and mirror neatly at the edge of bed. Change your position carefully.

PILLOW SCULPTRESS is struck by artistic inspiration early in the morning. Give her plenty of elbow room.

PHYSICAL CULTURIST wants to have her back massaged every night to ease her tensions—but not necessarily yours.

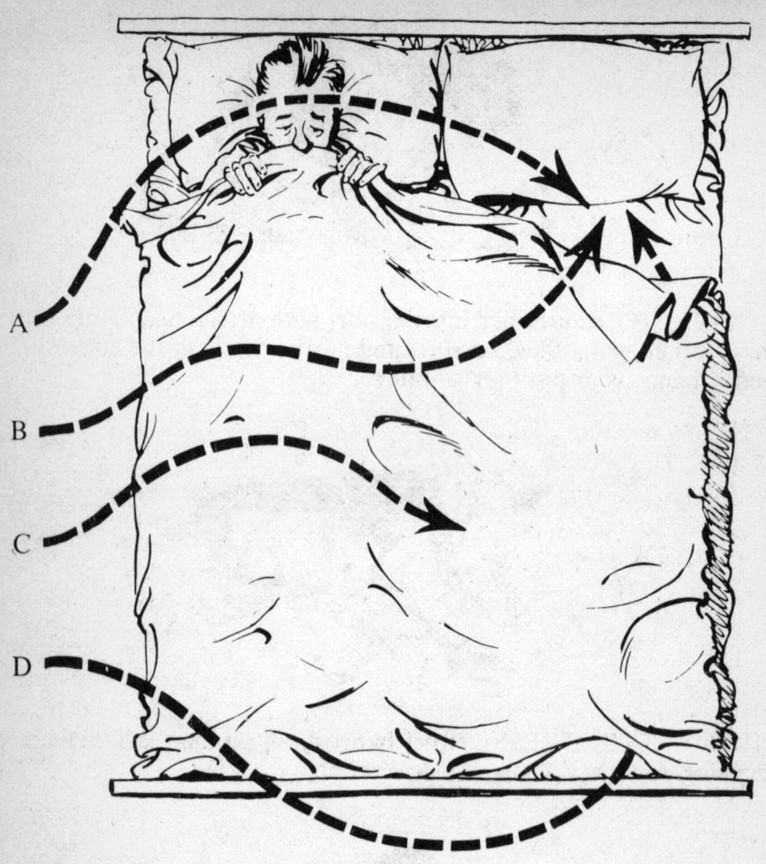

Trying not to disturb their husbands, wives use various ways to get back into bed. Stepping over face (A), brushing his nose ever so lightly, is among one of the favourites. Those who like to take short-cuts use direct route via stomach (B). Broadjump (C) is favoured by the more athletically inclined set—though husbands claim their wives tend to underestimate distances. Still another way to make a sudden—and unexpected—appearance next to husband is by means of digging a tunnel (D) under the blanket.

CHAPTER IV

AT HOME WITH A NEUROTIC WIFE

Occasionally, husbands return to their homes.

This happens when they have exhausted all possible alternatives. Short of cash and in need of a change of suit, they may not want to spend the night in a hotel room. Their friends no longer want to put them up for weeks at a time. The weather may be too cold to sleep on park benches. Bus stations are too noisy for a night's comfort.

Under these circumstances, it occurs to husbands that home, after all, is not without certain physical attractions; there are chairs, tables, closets, refrigerators, pillows, light bulbs, and toilet seats available to the visitor.

The problem is, of course, that married couples usually have the same address. Thus, there is a possibility that the wife may be there waiting when the husband comes home.

Anticipating his homecoming in the evening, most wives make an effort to look as attractive as they can for him. In this day and age, informality is the keynote in fashion. Shown here the three most popular at-home outfits as modelled by neurotic wives.

One of the responsibilities of a housewife is to keep her home neat. This feat cannot be accomplished without the husband's full cooperation, of course.

Fortunately, neurotic wives know how to get things done. They are outstanding administrators who know the art of delegating responsibilities. He washes the dishes and she inspects them. He takes out the garbage while she points the way at the door. He puts the clothes in the washing machine but she looks at the items carefully before allowing him to proceed with the chore of ironing.

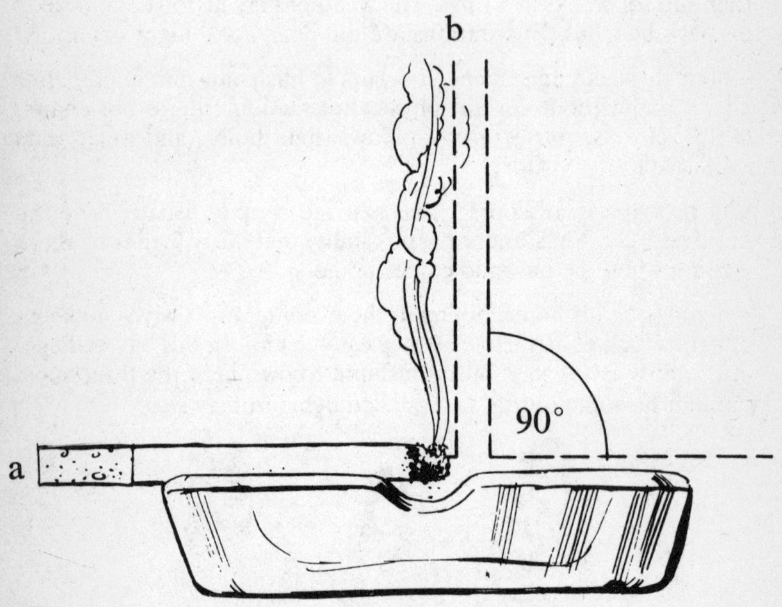

Well-trained husbands know how to keep order at home. Take smoking, for example. Fastidious wife will see to it that cigarette (a) on an ashtray lies perfectly *parallel* with the table. Smoke (b) rises *vertically* to please the eye. Smoker sits up *straight*, shoulders squared, looking *directly ahead*.

The mark of a good wife is that she keeps looking for ways to improve the appearance of a home. Furniture may be rearranged several times a year—the exercise helps husband's physical condition. Even if the room at the end looks the same as at the beginning of the year, the experience makes the effort worthwhile.

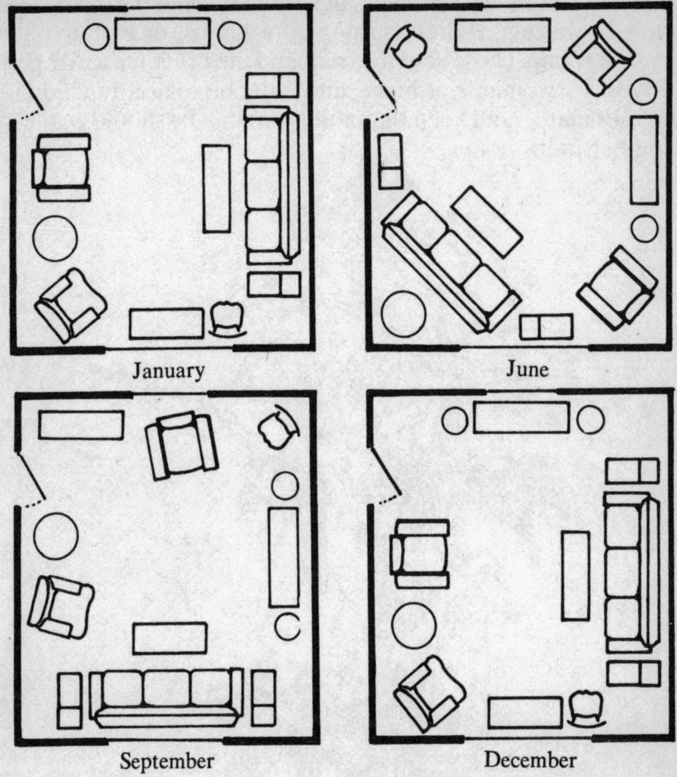

Critics of the modern social scene claim that the American male is relinquishing his masculine prerogatives.

This is not necessarily so.

The majority of wives in this country—within the confines of their home at least—are as eager as always to remain femininely passive, particularly when things have to be fixed.

In fact, the average neurotic wife makes a special effort to stay away from what she considers his domain; she not only concedes his superiority but actually goes out of her way in letting him know that it is a man's—not a woman's—job to maintain a home as a perfect place in which to live.

She is perfectly willing to prove to him, even if this means getting medical evidence, that the female anatomy is punily equipped for such heavy work as changing light bulbs, opening and closing windows, swatting at flies, turning door knobs, or carting pillows across the room. These activities demand the brute muscular power of a male. A woman's primary, and only, biological function is to please her man—and keep reminding him that he should be pleased having her in his home.

WORK AROUND THE HOUSE CONJURES UP A NEW—AND PROMISING—IMAGE OF HUSBAND IN A WIFE'S EYES. In her imagination she now sees him as an accomplished carpenter, plumber, TV repairman, landscape artist, ditchdigger, chimney sweeper, paper hanger, welder, bricklayer, electrician, road builder, farm hand, upholsterer, exterminator, strongman, and garbage collector—a man of great versatility who is willing to work without pay.

IT SOON BECOMES CLEAR TO THE WIFE THAT MAN'S EFFICIENCY DEPENDS MOSTLY ON HER ABILITY TO ORGANIZE HIS DAY. The following schedule laid out by a wife for her husband is typical:

4.30 a.m.	Get up. Don overalls.
4.45	Put shingles on roof. Do it quietly to keep from waking up household.
6.30	Paint house.
11.00	Take dog for a walk.
11.15	Build a garage.
12.30 p.m.	Eat breakfast
12.31	Wash car. Rotate tyres. Overhaul engine.
1.00	Transplant perennials from back yard to front lawn.
1.15	Transplant shrubs from front lawn to back yard.
1.30	Move perennials back to where they were in the first place.
3.00	Go the bathroom.
4.05	Give dog a bath.
4.30	Build a treehouse.
8.00	Have lunch.
8.01	Build a porch.
9.30	Give wife a back massage.
12.30 a.m.	Feed dog.
2.30	Wash overalls.
3.00	Go to bed.

Since men are usually home only after working hours, weekends, holidays, two weeks' vacation—or about 120 days out of 365—a wife may still find that at times she must carry on alone. All the same, she accepts her fate bravely. Here is a schedule of her day:

7.30 a.m.	Saying, "Good-bye, dear," to departing husband.
10.30	Going to the bathroom.
11.30	Thinking about getting up.
1.00 p.m.	Getting up.
1.15	Taking a shower.
1.30	Calling friends.
2.00	Going back to bed.
2.30	Making a cheese sandwich for lunch.
3.00	Turning on television.
4.30	Reminding husband about shopping on his way home.
5.00	Putting on makeup.
5.30	Calling friends.
6.30	Discussing dinner with husband at home.
7.30	Going to restaurant.
8.45	Attending a movie house.
11.00	Returning home.
11.01	Telling kids to keep quiet.
11.02	Turning on television.
3.00 a.m.	Turning off television.
3.01	Bedtime.

HOUSEWIFE'S ENERGY QUOTIENT (HEQ) is high. Here is what she can—and often does—accomplish in a *single* hour. From living room couch (1) she goes to bathroom (2). On her return trip, she walks past mirror (3) patting her hair in place, then straightens out pictures (4). She still has enough strength left to look out the window (5). At centre of the room (6) she comes to a halt to blow her nose. Turning knob on television set (7) she tries out armchair (8) but settles down on living room couch (1). Out of breath but as well as can be expected, she turns on table lamp (9) and calls (10) neighbour.

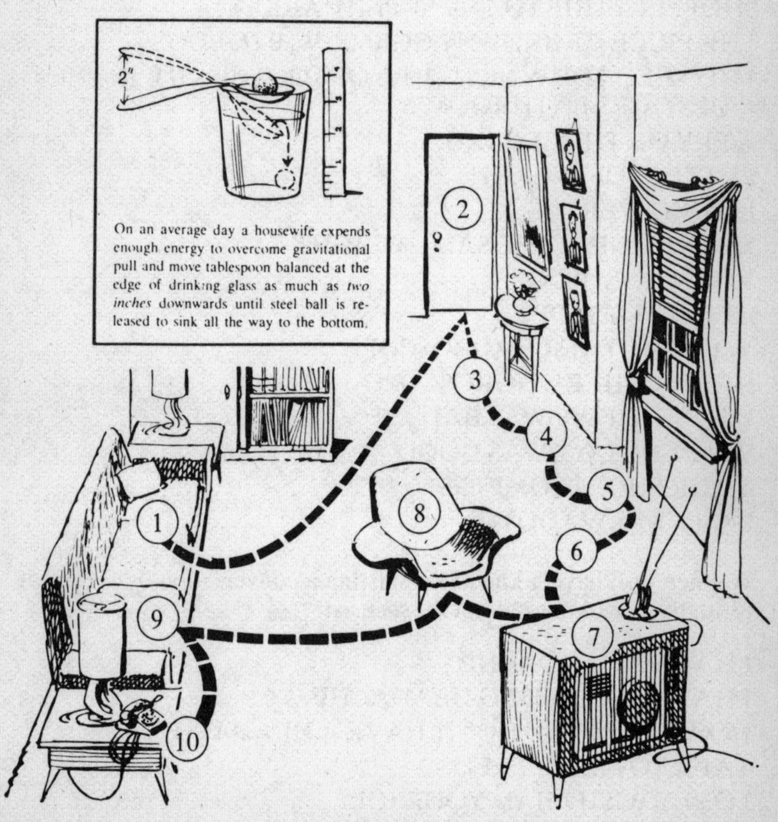

HOW TO CARRY ON A CONVERSATION WITH A NEUROTIC WIFE

It is impossible to be in same room with a neurotic wife for a long period—say, one minute—and not be drawn into a conversation. She will have more to say than you, of course, for hers is a more complete existence. Moreover, she is observant of details that fail to catch the attention of the average male. This is why wives find it so easy to carry on intelligent conversations on just about any subject. For example:

SHOPPING TRIP TO THE SUPERMARKET
THE PRICE OF BROWN EGGS VS. WHITE EGGS
THE NEED FOR A NEW TUBE OF TOOTHPASTE IN THE UPSTAIRS BATHROOM
A FLY ON THE CEILING
PUTTING ON WEIGHT
LOSING WEIGHT
MAINTAINING THE SAME WEIGHT
YOUR HOROSCOPE
HER HOROSCOPE
YOUR MOTHER'S HOROSCOPE
HER MOTHER'S HOROSCOPE
WHY THE DAY WAS BAD
WHY THE DAY WAS GOOD
YOUR SHORTCOMINGS
BABY'S NEW TOOTH

Women also have a knack for starting a conversation by means of thought-provoking statements such as:

I HAVE A HEADACHE.
I HAVE A SPLITTING HEADACHE.
HOW COME YOU DON'T HAVE A HEADACHE?
TALK TO ME, ALFRED.
I ONLY WISH I HAD YOUR JOB.
YOU DON'T UNDERSTAND WOMEN.
YOU THINK SEX IS EVERYTHING.
DO YOU THINK I'M SEXY?

Remarks like these can start a conversation if you don't watch out. You can forestall this possibility by the "Automatic Response Technique" which permits you to read a newspaper or catch up on your sleep while *committing you to absolutely nothing*. For example:

YES, DEAR.
IS THAT SO?
AND THEN WHAT HAPPENED?
YOU DON'T SAY!
HOW RIGHT YOU ARE.
YOU CERTAINLY HAVE WHAT IT TAKES.
SOME PEOPLE HAVE ALL THE LUCK.
THAT'S TELLING 'EM.
YOU CAN SAY THAT AGAIN.

The neurotic wife's capacity for talking for long periods of time *without stopping for breath* has attracted considerable scientific attention. It is the opinion of most zoologists that women have a respiratory apparatus unique to their species. Apparently, she does not inhale through her mouth and nose but absorbs oxygen through pores of her skin, especially in the area of the nape of her neck (1), earlobes (2), hands (3), knees (4), and toes (5). Air adjusts itself to body temperature (98.6°) and leaves through the mouth in form of a vaporous substance known as "hot air."

As story-tellers, women are without peers. They can describe events in a lucid, interesting style that is beyond achievement of the ordinary male.

HER VERSION

". . . and, oh yes, I forgot to tell you, or did I forget? I really don't know whether I did or not, but anyway, Grace came over this morning. I was having my usual cup of coffee with only one table-spoonful of sugar because of the calories, you know. Incidentally, you didn't notice. You never do. Anyway, as I said, Grace was wearing her Dynel wig. Isn't that awful? I know for a fact that her husband could certainly afford to buy her a wig made of human hair. Nobody should run around in a Dynel wig, at least not in this neighbourhood. Right? Anyway, Grace said, 'Good morning.' Just like that. Now I wasn't going to say anything about that awful hair-piece of hers. It's really none of my business. I simply asked her about her weight. We both follow the same diet, you know. And I'm entitled to know the truth. We're friends, you know. She told me she lost three pounds. Hah! She's a liar, of course. I have eyes. But I didn't say anything. I have brains, too. Besides, we are good friends. Hey, are you listening? That's the trouble with you men, you never listen."

HIS VERSION

Grace came over for a cup of coffee this morning.

Trying to get away from their wives, at least for a little while, some husbands use ingenious—if somewhat desperate—methods.

TREEHOUSE is for those who want to communicate with nature, not wife.

BALLOON leaves the ground quietly.

TUNNEL provides access to get-away car.

Man's ultimate sanctuary is his bathroom. Here he can enjoy a sense of privacy not available anywhere else in the house, except possibly the living room closet. Bathroom can be equipped for overnight stay. Pillow (1), headrest (2), footstool (3) provide comfort. Lamp (4) supplies light for reading. Built-in television set (5) and telephone (6) help occupant to keep in touch. Medicine cabinet (7) holds liquor and other provisions. Roller skates and dumb-bells (8) are for exercise. Deck of cards (9) are for playing solitaire, chips (10) are for betting on oneself. Double lock (11) keeps out intruders.

CHAPTER V

THE BABY AND HIS NEUROTIC MOTHER

About the time you learn to cope with your neurotic wife, you will have to face a new set of trying circumstances. Amidst appropriate fanfare, the baby will arrive. With that, any hope you might have had of being head of the household will disappear overnight.

Your baby may have your eyes, your grandfather's nose, and your great-grandfather's ears, but his personality will be that of his mother. This will become particularly obvious during his periods of temper tantrums.

The allegiance between baby and his mother is unspoken but nevertheless the strongest bond in nature. It can withstand external pressure of all sorts, and any that emanates from you. There exists an extraordinary singleness of purpose between the child and his mother; namely, to put you in your place, to set you back for good.

It takes an average infant only a few minutes to find out exactly where he stands. His formal education may be incomplete at his age but he makes up for his lack of information with plenty of common sense. Not only is he able to size up his position correctly, but *yours* as well. This gives him self-confidence to deal with you. The opportunities to annoy you appear to be unlimited.

From his mother, he soon learns his rights: to scream any time he wants and as loudly as his oversized lungs will allow. Mother will accept his wailing as a form of healthy self-expression and will turn the task of quietening the baby over to you. He will sense your utter helplessness and put his vocal cords to the test over and over again. Your wife will then scream at you for not being able to stop the baby from screaming and this will make you scream back at her. The noise will amuse the offspring, making him kick up his heels in joy.

Episodes like this will go a long way toward helping him to understand the Authority Structure of a Modern Family. And he will keep things going his way as long as possible—say, about fifteen to twenty years.

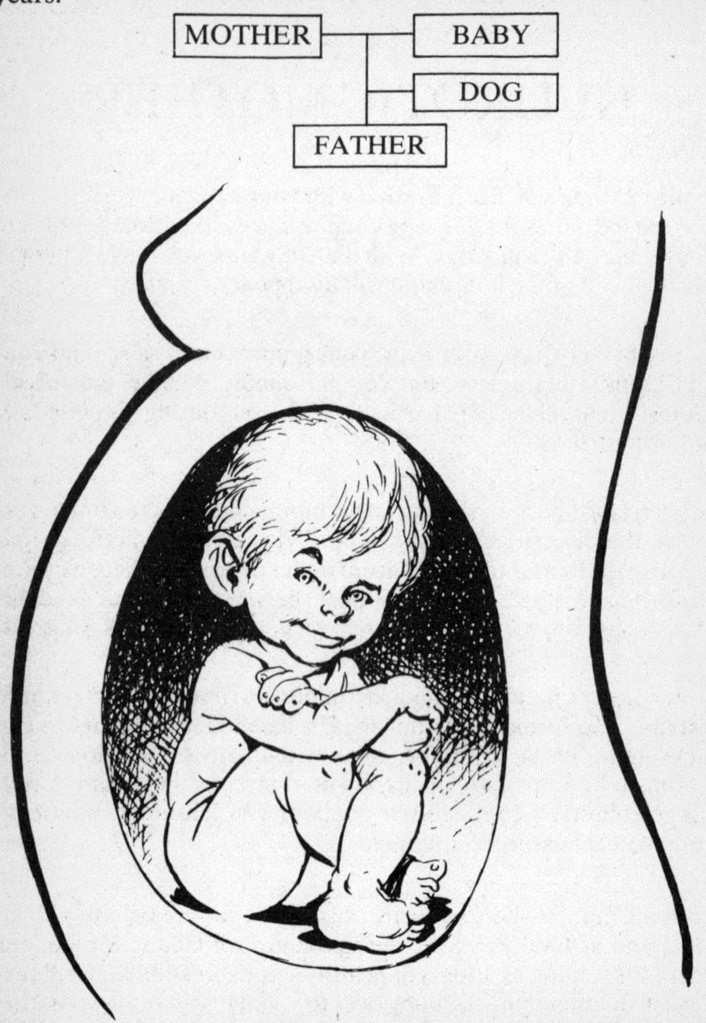

In his mother's womb, baby has an opportunity to eavesdrop on conversations between parents. He soon learns who has the last word. Laughing to himself, his body shakes. His quaking can clearly be felt by his mother, who will refer to his movements as "kicking".

Baby experiences his first serious trauma when getting his first glimpse of his father. He finds it difficult to believe that such a man should be part of his family. Told that this is the case and there is nothing he can do about it at this point, he lets out a howl. It may take him a lifetime to overcome the initial shock of meeting his father.

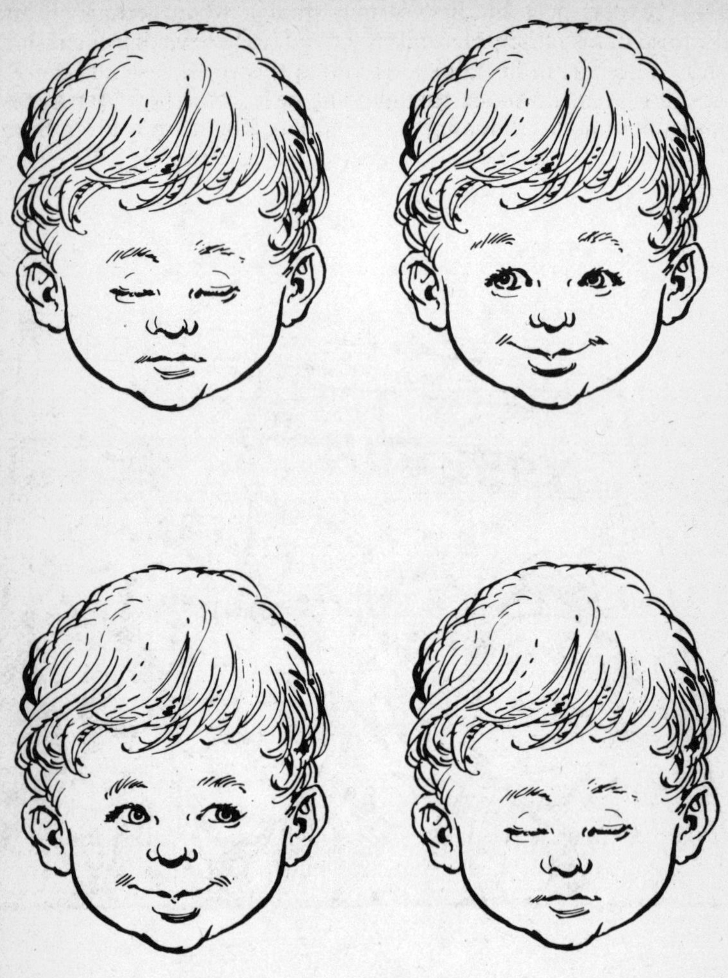

In his nursery at home, baby regards his father's antics with a sidelong glance from his vantage point, the crib. He may feign sleep but nothing escapes his attention. He finds his father's ponderous attempts not to awaken him especially entertaining.

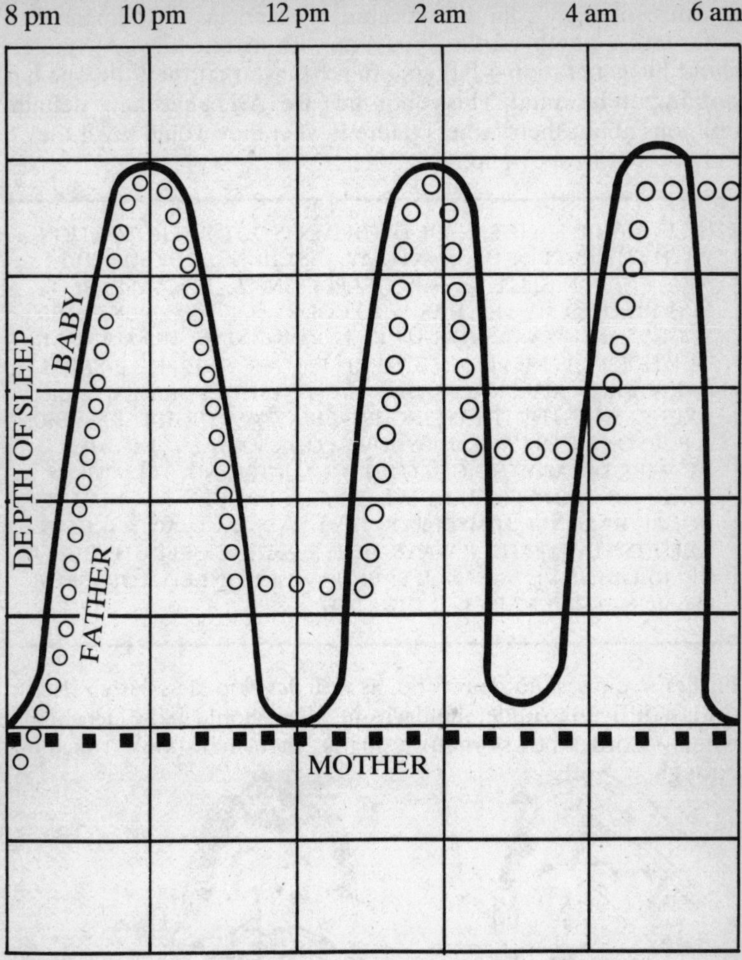

SLEEPING CHART shows correlation of sleeping patterns in the same household. When baby awakes and startles the world with a scream, father responds to the sound by leaping out of bed. He runs to the crib. This pleases baby and he goes back to sleep. Father goes back to bed. Performance is repeated several times in the course of the night. Then, in the small hours of the morning, baby decides to catch up on his sleep while father waits nervously in his bed for the next rallying cry. Mother sleeps through the night and wakes up refreshed.

Because of baby's limited vocabulary—and his unwillingness to enter into a lengthy, futile discussion with anyone too old to understand his generation—fathers often believe that the little one has nothing on his mind. This is not the case. All babies have definite opinions about their fathers. Here is what they would say if they'd only bother to speak up:

HE IS BIG BUT THE SIZE OF HIS BRAIN IS OUT OF PROPORTION WITH THE REST OF HIS ANATOMY. HIS CHANCES OF SURVIVAL ARE FAIR IN SPITE OF HIS HELPLESSNESS, BECAUSE HE IS MARRIED TO MY MOTHER WHO COOKS FOR HIM, MENDS HIS SOCKS, AND WAKES HIM UP IN THE MORNING. HIS MANUAL DEXTERITY IS NIL. I CAN BITE HIS FINGER WHEN HE INSERTS PACIFIER IN MY MOUTH (HA, HA, HA). HIS VOICE IS DEEP, EXCEPT WHEN I BITE HIS FINGER. IT BECOMES HIGH THEN. FOR A PERSON OF HIS AGE, HE SHOWS POOR SOCIAL JUDGEMENT. HE WILL DO ANYTHING TO GET A LAUGH: SING, TELL JOKES, FLAIL HIS ARMS PRETENDING TO FLY, DANCE AROUND THE ROOM, BALANCE HIMSELF ON HIS HEAD—AND ACT LIKE AN IDIOT IN MANY OTHER WAYS. HE IS SHOWING DEFINITE SIGNS OF REGRESSIVE INFANTILE BEHAVIOUR. NEED FOR PROFESSIONAL THERAPY IS INDICATED.

Father's sense of humour is not as well developed as baby's. Infant finds it difficult to understand why his elder should make faces at him when—Lord knows—nature made that man look ridiculous enough.

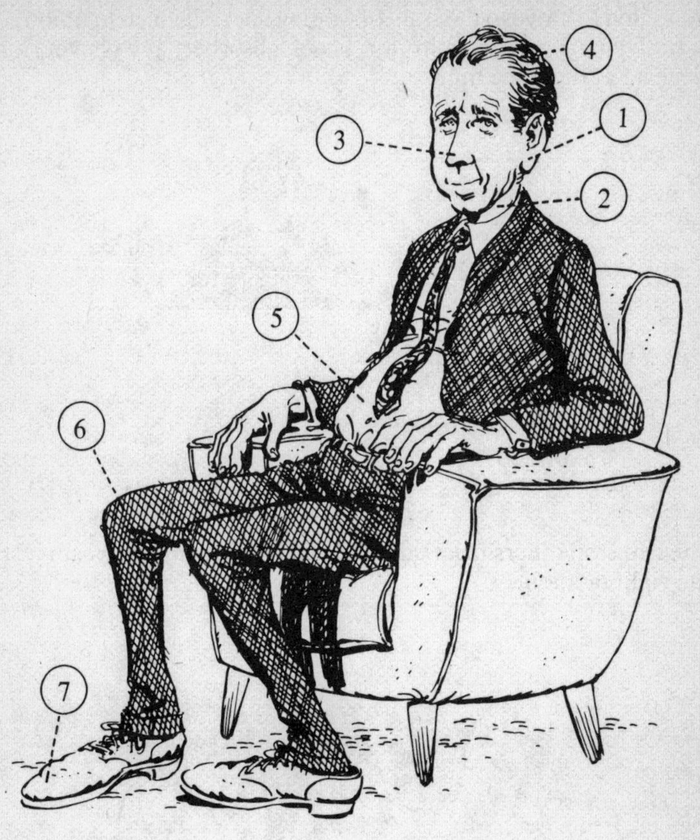

Baby sees his father not only as a supplier of such economic necessities as rattles and wood blocks but himself a huge and well-made toy. Fathers come complete with such useful appurtenances as earlobes (1) to be rolled into small balls, neck (2) to be twisted into pretzel-shape, nose (3) to bite into, tufts of hair (4) to gather up in one's tiny fists, a protruding belly (5) on which to jump up and down for hours at a time, knees (6) to ride on, and toes (7) to step on.

Wives often take baby along for practical reasons. The ploy makes it possible for them to get seats on buses, cross streets against red lights, be invited to move to the front of waiting lines. Their companion acts as bodyguard, social arbitrator, shock absorber, and conversation piece all at the same time.

She can stop others from talking by inducing baby to scream just at the right moment.

She can have baby inspect opponent's cards.

On the dance floor, baby can be used to keep partner at a distance.

Baby can be trained to interrupt any activity at any time.

CHAPTER VI

THE NEUROTIC WORKING WIFE

Not all neurotic wives are working but all working wives are neurotic.

That's because when employed, a woman must change her whole pattern of life and, most importantly, her sleeping schedule. The traumatic experience of changing her routine leaves her emotionally exhausted, making her neurotic.

In some cases she may even have to get up in the morning the same time as her husband.

Moreover, once out of bed and in the office, her opportunities to take quick, two- to three-hour catnaps are curtailed, save for occasional trips to the powder room where she can lie down on a couch or the floor, or to the conference room where she may unobtrusively doze off with her eyes open while taking notes.

Noise level in most offices is high. There are sounds of typewriters, footsteps, telephones, and voices of executives trying to get her attention.

No arrangements are made to provide continuous entertainment, either. Christmas parties are an exception but, in most corporations, they are only held once a year. And there are no television sets, movie screens, musical groups, not even a jukebox—nothing to keep employees awake.

All coffee breaks are too short.

So are the hours for lunch.

And yet—despite their hostile environment—working wives keep on working because they know what they want.

She knows that there is no better way to put you down.

She can now bring home a paycheque which looks very much like yours. She is free to wave it before your eyes, read it out loud, fold it into paper planes, or do with it anything she pleases. There is nothing you can do but stand by and hope that the day will come when discrimination between the sexes will come to an end, and you will be permitted to speak up.

I'LL SHOW HIM.
I'LL SHOW THAT MISERABLE MISOGYNIST.
I DIDN'T GO TO COLLEGE FOR NOTHING.
JUST BECAUSE I'M A WOMAN, IT DOESN'T MEAN I CAN'T BE SOMEBODY.
I CAN TAKE ON ANY MAN IN THE HOUSE.
I'VE GOT TO DO MY THING.
THEY'VE GOT TO PAY ME.
WHY SHOULD HE MAKE ALL THE MONEY?
I WANT MY RIGHTS.
THEY NEED ME.
WHO SAYS IT'S A MAN'S WORLD?
I WANT TO IMPROVE MYSELF.
MY GIRLFRIENDS MAY BE DUMB BUT NOT ME.
I'M NOT ONLY A BEAUTIFUL GIRL BUT A SMART ONE AT THAT.
AND WHY SHOULDN'T THERE BE A WOMAN RUNNING FOR PRESIDENT?
I'M NOT COMPETITIVE AS LONG AS NOBODY GETS AHEAD OF ME.

Contrary to popular belief, wives do not work for money alone. Theirs is a desire to make a contribution to the world and they're just as good as the next fellow.

There are deep-seated, psychological forces that make wives compete with men. Studies indicate that career women refuse to accept the role of passivity thrust upon them in their early childhood lasting thirty or forty years.

INABILITY TO VAULT AS HIGH AS HER BROTHER brings to her attention anatomical differences between sexes.

AS A LOSER IN A BARROOM FIGHT, she learns that her arm reach is shorter than men's.

REJECTED BY THE UNITED STATES ARMY RECONNAISSANCE FORCE, her ego suffers another blow.

At times, the average working wife finds that her superiority in business is being questioned by men. This is another reason why she must fight harder.

She soon realises that in the world of business, men have all the advantages.

For one thing, they are bigger and more powerful. This enables them to bang on tables more effectively and carry larger, more impressive briefcases to and from their work. Men are also more agile at footwork. They can put their feet on the desk.

All this only proves to the woman that she must live by her wits alone. Her only chance for survival is to develop techniques all her own, aimed to confuse her male adversaries.

She has no trouble in doing just that. Freely substituting opinions for facts whenever the need arises, and calling this "common sense approach", she succeeds in making everybody think she has a particular gift in getting to the heart of the matter. Since most of her male associates are married and know the futility of arguing with a woman, she usually has no trouble getting her way.

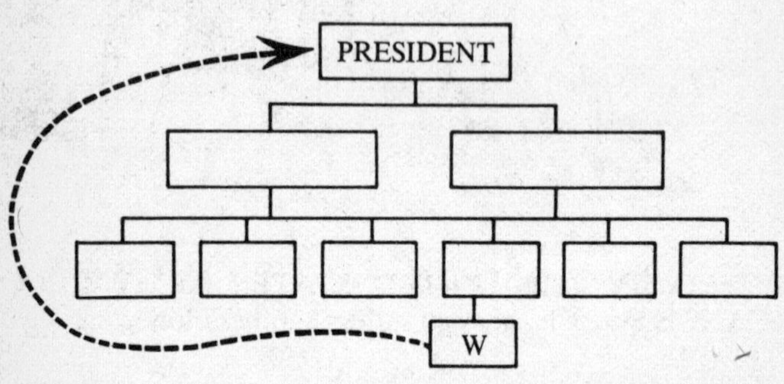

Woman has a genius to do away with red tape. The concept of organisational structure is much too abstract for her taste; she prefers to take a direct route wherever she wants to go. To get to the president, for example, becomes a matter of simply walking up to his office.

THE PRESIDENT

The chief executive officer of the corporation. His duties include all managerial and executive functions in connection with the office of President and the devotion of all his skill, knowledge, and abilities in the furtherance of his business.

Corporate Definition

THE PRESIDENT

A short, chubby man wearing elevated shoes. Nearsighted. Overweight. Bald. Keeps tranquillisers, aspirin, bars of candy, and back issues of *Playboy* in his desk drawer. His wife calls every afternoon to check up on him. Likes to have his back massaged.

Woman's Definition

Woman's definition of the President differs significantly from that of the Corporation.

A woman's office reflects her personality. Feminine touch in decor is to remind visitors that they are in the presence of a delicate creature in need of special treatment.

Dinner at home with a working spouse—if she gets home at all in the evenings—calls for good listening habits. There is much she has to tell after a hard day's work in the office.

Most career women prefer dinner tables which have seating arrangements with them clearly at the head. This makes them the centre of attention and keeps everyone else in the family facing them while she holds forth.

There may be a question-and-answer period after dinner.

Shape of table popular with working wives sharing a meal with the family.

"JOHN, YOU WOULDN'T BELIEVE THIS BUT TODAY WAS ABSOLUTELY THE WORST. YOU REMEMBER WHEN I TOLD YOU I ASKED FOR A WHITE TELEPHONE? THAT WAS LAST WEEK. AND GUESS WHAT HAPPENED TODAY. NOTHING. YES, NOTHING. I'VE BEEN WAITING FOR THAT TELEPHONE FOR I DON'T KNOW HOW LONG. AND TODAY, I WENT TO WORK FOR THE SOLE PURPOSE OF WAITING SOME MORE. I ASKED THEM. YOU KNOW, ABOUT THE WHITE TELEPHONE. AND THEY SAID, TAKE IT EASY. THE PHONE COMPANY CAN AFFORD TO TAKE ITS TIME. AND I SAID, 'OKAY, LET'S CALL AND ASK THEM.' THEY SAID, 'GO RIGHT AHEAD, YOU CALL THEM.' SO I DID. ON MY BLACK TELEPHONE. AND THE PHONE PEOPLE SAID, 'WE'LL HAVE YOUR TELEPHONE NEXT WEEK.' IMAGINE THAT! IT TAKES A BIG COMPANY THAT LONG TO COME UP WITH A TINY LITTLE WHITE TELEPHONE. ISN'T THAT SOMETHING? AND YOU WONDER WHY I LOOK SO TIRED IN THE EVENINGS."

Working wife's typical reply to husband's polite inquiry: "And how was your day in the office, dear?"

Even more important than dinner is breakfast to the working wife. This is her opportunity to unveil the Plan of Action for the day.

All professional women know only too well what awaits them in an office. They are wise to the fact that behind every desk, filing cabinet, and watercooler lurks the enemy determined to bring their progress in business to a halt.

Figure about an hour for breakfast.

Make sure the table is set before she makes an entrance. Her favourite juice should be there, be it orange, grapefruit, tomato, or bourbon-on-the-rocks.

Make an earnest effort to stay awake during her soliloquy.

Ultimately, a working wife's husband must bid farewell to his outward-bound spouse. Try hiding your true feelings when this occurs. Demonstrate your devotion to her as long as she is inside that door and she sees you.

THROW HER A KISS | SOB UNCONTROLLABLY | WISH HER GOOD LOOK

CHAPTER VII

HOW TO MAKE A NEUROTIC WIFE FEEL RELAXED

If your wife yells at you, throws herself on the floor and beats the ground with her fist, she is trying to tell you something.

You should be able to recognise symptoms of inner tension—minor as they may seem to you at a superficial glance—and make an effort to help her. That means more than just calling an ambulance and carting her away. It means that you must learn to show sympathy.

She probably has every reason to be upset. Hers is a difficult life. Her days are filled with crises which she must solve all by herself. Crises like running out of hairpins, breaking a pencil point, discovering lack of salt in the tomato soup, losing a paper napkin.

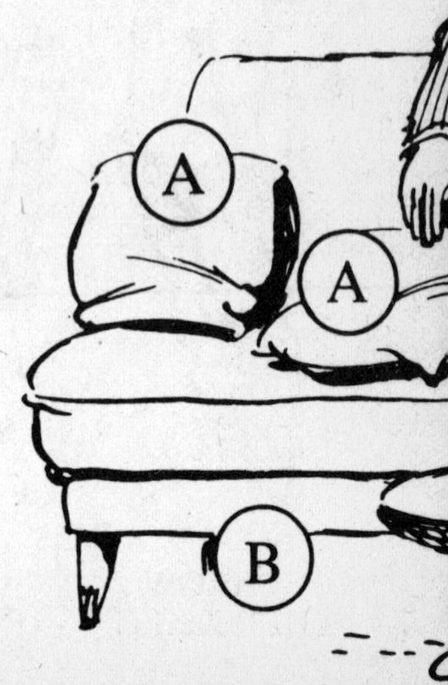

Nothing is as important in a marriage as reassuring your wife that you love her even though you're married to her. There are husbands who would rather tell the truth but they risk being sued for a divorce. To make her feel wanted, you must show your devotion by way of small, but meaningful, presents such as a miniature gold wristwatch, a tiny pair of diamond earrings, or just a plain teeny-weeny custom-made sports car imported from Europe.

More than for anything, however, women hunger for sincerity on your part. They want you to pour your feelings into spoken words. To solve this dilemma, many husbands hire professional ghost writers to prepare material for them and then put this on a tape recorder. The machine can be kept out of sight and all the husband has to do is mouth the words while the message is being delivered.

PLACES TO HIDE THE TAPE RECORDER. (A) Behind pillows. (B) Under the couch. (C) Inside the flower pot. (D) In your nostrils.

Be generous with praise. Every woman likes to be complimented now and then.

One of the best ways to get rid of frustrations is to follow a regular physical fitness programme. Especially popular among women are isometric exercises. These can be performed indoors without her ever leaving the couch. Make sure she starts out slowly at first to get in shape and work *gradually* toward a more strenuous routine, that is, ten to fifteen seconds of workout such as shown below.

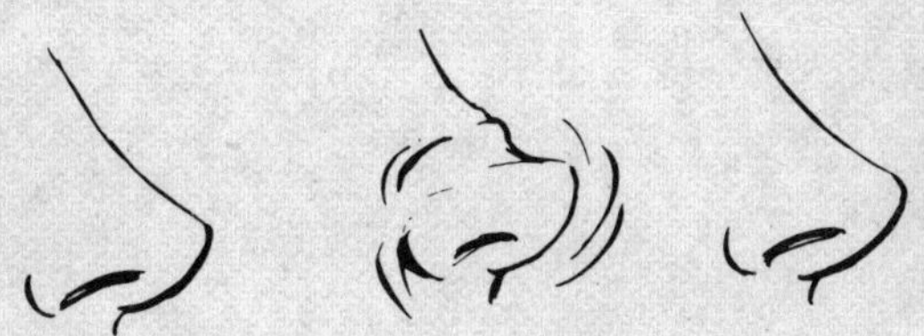

NOSE TWITCHING relaxes olfactory senses.

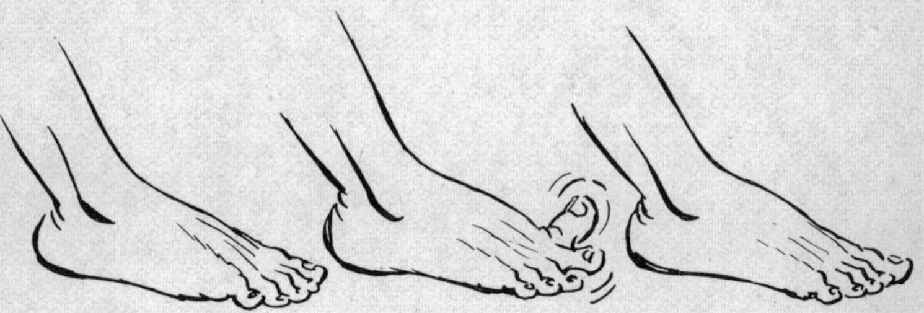

TOE CALISTHENICS stimulate blood circulation at the very tip of the human anatomy.

EYEBROW RAISING strengthens forehead muscles.

Darkened room soothes her nerves. Turn off lights, pull down shades, close curtains tightly. Now she won't see you leaving.

Drinking in moderation boosts her morale—and yours.

From ancient Hindu philosophers comes a mystical philosophy called Yoga. It involves withdrawal from the World, represented by you, and abstract meditation upon any object, such as the Supreme Spirit, represented by her. Persuade your wife to try it. Particularly effective is the headstand; it makes talking difficult if not impossible. Have her maintain this posture for several hours.

If everything else fails, be a sport. Entertain your wife.

Sing to her.

Greensleeves

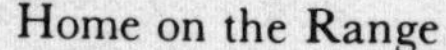

Home on the Range

G C

Oh, give me a home, where the buf - fa - lo roam, Where the

G A7 D7

deer and the an - te - lope play, Where

G C

sel - dom is heard a dis - cour - ag - ing word, And the

G D7 G

skies are not cloud - y all day.

Chorus

G D7 G

Home, home on the range, Where the

Em A7 D7

deer and the an - te - lope play, Where

G C

sel - dom is heard a dis - cour - ag - ing word, And the

G D7 G

skies are not cloud - y all day.

Read her a bedtime story.

Poems
of
Romance

SOME OF HER FAVOURITE STORIES:

Little Miss Muffet
Sat on a tuffet,
Eating her curds and whey.
There came a big spider,
Who sat down beside her,
And frightened Miss Muffet away.

Curly locks, Curly locks,
    Wilt thou be mine?
Thou shalt not wash dishes
    Nor yet feed the swine,
But sit on a cushion
    And sew a fine seam,
And feed upon strawberries,
    Sugar and cream.

Lavender's blue, diddle, diddle,
    Lavender's green;
When I am king, diddle, diddle,
    You shall be queen.

Humpty Dumpty sat on a wall,
Humpty Dumpty had a great fall.
    All the king's horses,
    And all the king's men,
Couldn't put Humpty together again.

Little miss, pretty miss,
    Blessings light upon you!
If I had half a crown a day,
    I'd spend it all upon you.

Mary had a little lamb;
    Its fleece was white as snow;
And everywhere that Mary went
    The lamb was sure to go.

It followed her to school one day,
    That was against the rule;
It made the children laugh and play
    To see a lamb at school.

And so the teacher turned it out,
    But still it lingered near;
And waited patiently about
    Till Mary did appear.

"Why does the lamb love Mary so?"
    The eager children cry.
"Why, Mary loves the lamb, you know,"
    The teacher did reply.

There was a little girl, and she had a little curl
    Right in the middle of her forehead;
When she was good, she was very, very good,
    But when she was bad, she was horrid.

What are little boys made of, made of?
What are little boys made of?
"Snips and snails, and puppy-dogs' tails;
And that's what little boys are made of, made of."

What are little girls made of, made of?
What are little girls made of?
"Sugar and spice, and all that's nice;
And that's what little girls are made of, made of."

CHAPTER VIII

HOW TO GET RID OF A NEUROTIC WIFE

The question most often asked by husbands concerned with the emotional health of their beloved wives is "Yes, but how do I get rid of her?"

The situation would improve at once, husbands say, if participation in a marriage were narrowed down to only one person at a time.

This concept, however, meets with opposition by the wives. It's not that she objects to keeping the number of participants to a minimum; it is only that she thinks you are the one who should leave.

The law is on their side. Elimination of a wife brings about a multitude of jurisprudential problems payable by the husband. Our marriage laws are based on old-fashioned Puritan traditions. They have not yet caught up with the pace of modern times. For example, to shoot a wife in public or even in the privacy of a home is illegal. Similarly, it is considered unconstitutional in this country to give an overdose of sleeping pills to the wife even though she may complain of insomnia; put arsenic in her coffee cup even if this is to improve the taste; place a time-bomb inside an anniversary cake even though that makes for good filling; or lovingly embrace her in such a way that she is choked into oblivion.

It should also be remembered that law enforcement agents are particularly astute in solving matrimonial crimes since most of them are married men themselves and understand perfectly your motives that led you to do away with your wife. Thus it is possible that you would get caught.

A more acceptable way to remove your wife from your immediate vicinity is by means of a lawyer. The cost of legal assistance, however, is higher than that of sleeping pills, arsenic, and time-bomb combined. Time to an attorney is a valuable commodity, convertible to cash.

He will probably be the first one to admit that getting a divorce is expensive, and prove his point by sending you a large bill for having made that statement.

Marriage counsellors charge less for their services but they do not like to get to the core of the problem; namely, your wife. Instead, they have both parties appear in their offices so that they can air their differences, vastly entertaining the counsellor. A marriage counsellor can save your marriage. But that is exactly what you are trying to avoid.

Generally speaking, a psychoanalyst—if you can afford him—is more sympathetic to your plight, for he probably has problems with his own wife. For an hourly rate of twenty-five dollars or more, he will listen to your woes and periodically nod his head either in agreement or in his slumber. He may even provide a couch for you to lie down for forty-five minutes so you too can go to sleep. The couch may be covered with Morocco leather or vinyl, depending on the fee.

The therapy may take years, because psychoanalysts do not believe in rushing anything for which they get amply paid. After the first hundred sessions or so you will be told of striking similarities between your mother and the girl you have married; that is, that they are both women. This may not help you to dispose of your incumbent spouse, but as a piece of information, it certainly has interest.

In view of the foregoing, it would seem that the best way to get rid of a wife is to make her get rid of you. Admittedly, this calls for an effort on your part but, considering the size of the reward, it is certainly worth a try. The following pages suggest means by which you can make your wife realise that her life would be more complete without you.

PROVOCATION No. 1 Sing happily under the shower with the door open.

PROVOCATION No. 2 Make love at 4.30 a.m.

PROVOCATION No. 3 Show her in the family album a photograph taken of her in a bathing suit twenty years ago.

PROVOCATION No. 4 Throw a stag party in the living room.

SURE, I STILL LOVE YOU.

YOU CERTAINLY KNOW HOW TO MAKE THE MOST OF WHAT YOU'VE GOT.

OH, YOU SHAVED THIS MORNING!

JUST GOT YOU AN INFORMATIVE BOOK ON "SEX IN MARRIAGE".

HONEY, YOU LOOK JUST LIKE MY BROTHER.

I'D PREFER TO MAKE LOVE WITH THE LIGHTS OFF.

YOU LOOK SO BEAUTIFUL I HARDLY KNOW IT'S YOU.

MY, MY, WHAT A POWERFUL HANDSHAKE YOU HAVE.

YOU SMELL SO DIFFERENT. DID YOU HAVE A SHOWER, DEAR?

THAT GIRDLE DOES WONDERS FOR YOUR FIGURE.

YOUR RED DRESS MATCHES PERFECTLY THE COLOUR OF YOUR NOSE.

DON'T WORRY ABOUT IT, DEAR. WOMEN DON'T HAVE TO BE SMART.

YOU'RE GROWING OLD EVER SO GRACEFULLY.

I LIKE MATURITY IN A WOMAN.

PROVOCATION No. 5 **Insult her with compliments.**

One of the socially most acceptable ways to do away with a wife is to put her on a starvation diet. Through eating less and less, she thins gradually until the day when she disappears altogether.

To encourage your wife to lose weight, you must, of course, first convince her that she is too heavy. Tell her she would look more beautiful if only she would lose a few hundred pounds here and there.

Shown here is the most effective diet ever devised for husbands who want to see their spouse fade away altogether. Called the ABSOLUTE STARVATION DIET, it is based on the theory that the fewer the calories, the less the wife.

MONDAY

Breakfast Crab paste (one teaspoon) .... 10 calories
Mayonnaise (one teaspoon) .... 7 calories
Lunch Bottle of meatsauce .... 10 calories
Dinner Horse radish (one teaspoon) .... 5 calories
Chinese Cabbage .... 14 calories
Wheat germ .... 15 calories
Catsup (one teaspoon) .... 15 calories
TOTAL .... *76 calories*

TUESDAY

Breakfast Escarole (four small leaves) .... 4 calories
Lemon (one teaspoon) .... 15 calories
Catsup (one teaspoon) .... 15 calories
Lunch Raw Onions .... 4 calories
Green Peppers .... 15 calories
Dinner Canned Spinach .... 10 calories
Vanilla Extract (one teaspoon) .... 3 calories
Catsup (one teaspoon) .... 15 calories
TOTAL .... *81 calories*

WEDNESDAY

Breakfast Watercress (ten sprigs) .... 2 calories
Catsup (one teaspoon) .... 15 calories

Lunch Chopped Parsley (one teaspoon) .... 1 calorie
Soy Sauce (one teaspoon) .... 10 calories

Dinner Cheese Crackers .... 15 calories

TOTAL .... *43 calories*

THURSDAY

Breakfast Soda Seltzer .... 5 calories

Lunch Catsup (one teaspoon) .... 15 calories

Dinner Bouillon Cubes (beef or chicken) .... 2 calories

TOTAL .... *22 calories*

FRIDAY

Breakfast Black coffee .... No calories

Lunch Catsup (half teaspoon) .... 7½ calories

Dinner Mustard .... No calories

TOTAL .... *7½ calories*

SATURDAY

Breakfast Tea .... No calories

Lunch Mint .... 1 calorie

Dinner Herbs .... No calories

TOTAL .... *1 calorie*

SUNDAY

Breakfast Water (one glass) .... No calories

Lunch Water (one glass) .... No calories

Dinner Water (two glasses) .... No calories

TOTAL .... *No calories*

Your wife at the beginning of the month. | Your wife at the middle of the month. | Your wife at the end of the month.

THE ABSOLUTE STARVATION DIET: How it works.

Another way to eliminate your wife in a polite manner is to persuade her that happiness is not only living together but *playing* together. Like this:

RUSSIAN ROULETTE

KNIFE-THROWING

BREATH HOLDING CONTEST

LOVER'S LEAP. (LADIES ALWAYS GO FIRST)

PERSUADE HER TO GO TO THE MOON

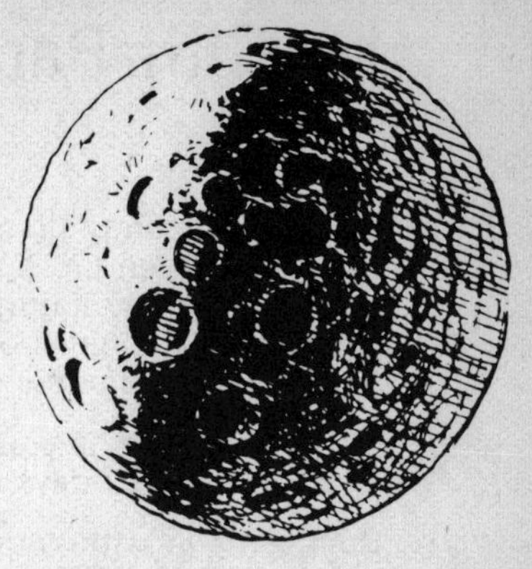

HOW TO AVOID FLYING
by Cliff Parker

Afeared of flying? If so, remember that statistics prove that forty-seven times more people die of old age in airport departure lounges than are hurt in crashes. Yet unbelievably, airlines only demonstrate survival techniques to the few who actually get on a plane.

This book, then, is your survival kit for use during those long bleak days and nights, waiting for take off.

Just settle in with your week's supply of packed lunches among the rows of untenanted car rental booths and banks closed till tomorrow, and read.

Don't worry about the flight. It will probably never happen. Scheduled or charter, if it's going to somewhere desirable it will be cancelled due to air traffic controllers/baggage handlers/cabin staff strikes. The only ones that actually get away are those going to places like Abu Dhabi that no one in their right mind would want to go to anyway.

When you've finished the book you can go home, refreshed, happy and safe.